FOR A MIRACLE

WHEN IT'S TIME FOR A MIRACLE

THE HOUR OF IMPOSSIBLE BREAKTHROUGHS IS NOW!

by

Lynne Hammond

Harrison House
Tulsa, Oklahoma

06 05 04 03   10 9 8 7 6 5 4 3 2

When It's Time for a Miracle—
The Hour of Impossible Breakthroughs is Now!
ISBN 1-57794-393-7 (formerly ISBN 1-57794-279-5)
Copyright © 2001 by Lynne Hammond
Mac Hammond Ministries
P.O. Box 29469
Minneapolis, Minnesota 55429

Published by Harrison House, Inc.
P.O. Box 35035
Tulsa, Oklahoma 74153

CONTENTS

INTRODUCTION

Before you start reading this book, I'd like you to take a moment to think of some impossibility in your life.

If there is turmoil in your family, the thought of peace and unity in your home may seem like a complete impossibility to you. Perhaps you're dealing with a physical condition that medical science says is impossible to cure. Or maybe God has called you to do something that seems impossible, and you have no idea how to go about fulfilling that divine assignment.

Whatever impossibilities you may be facing, I have some very good news for you: God delights in making impossibilities *possible!*

He was the God of the impossible for Moses and the Israelites when He parted the Red Sea and delivered them from their enemies. (Ex. 14:21-31.) He was the God of the impossible when He caused the sun to stand still so Joshua could lead his army on to victory. (Josh. 10:12,13.) He was certainly the God of the impossible when He raised Jesus from the dead. And He is still the very same God of the impossible in these last days before Jesus returns!

So as you read this little book, get ready to move on up to a higher level in God. God is calling you to that higher place, because only there will you learn to look every impossibility square in the face and declare with the boldness born of faith:

Impossibility, in Jesus' name I call you possible! It shall come to pass by the power of the Holy Ghost!

—Lynne Hammond

So pray to the Lord of the harvest to force

out and thrust laborers into His harvest.

MATTHEW 9:38

1

THE LAST-DAYS
OPERATION OF *SEND*

1

THE LAST-DAYS
OPERATION OF *SEND*

If you're a member of the body of Christ,
you are living in the midst of something *big*—
much bigger than you could ever imagine in
your own natural mind. Surrounding you is a
huge network of individual callings and gifts,
all designed to work together toward the
fulfillment of God's plans and purposes for
these last days.

> SURROUNDING YOU IS A HUGE NETWORK OF INDIVIDUAL CALLINGS AND GIFTS.

Over the years, I've discovered so many facets to this last-days move of God we are experiencing. Some people emphasize the rain, or the outpouring of the Holy Spirit, that God sends to bring in the great end-time harvest of souls. Other people emphasize miracles, signs and wonders. But a few years ago during a time of prayer, God revealed another very important facet of this divine move to me.

Fishers of Men

At the time, our church had a little downtown prayer mission where we would go pray every day for revival and for the city. One night we were down at the mission praying with one particular Scripture as our focus: **Pray ye therefore the Lord of the harvest, that he will send forth labourers into his harvest** (Matt. 9:38 KJV). That Scripture was a burning desire in my heart as I prayed in tongues. At one point I spoke out in English, "Pray ye therefore the Lord of the harvest, that he will *send*...."

When I got to that word "send," something just resounded and shook in my spirit man. Then the Lord spoke to my heart and said,

> SEND IS A MOTIVATING PLAN OF GOD FOR THE LAST DAYS.

The operation of send *is a motivating plan of God for the last days; it will thrust forth and hurl multitudes of people like missiles into the harvest fields of the world.*

You know, when man sends you out, there isn't much power. But when *God* sends you forth, it's a different thing altogether!

The Lord continued, saying, *I will make you fishers of men.* Then He showed me a big net He is in the process of weaving. The net is made up of people, and He is getting ready to throw it over all the earth. In this huge, invisible net—this operation of *send*—every person has a part. In fact, I can't begin to describe to you all the different facets and parts I saw in God's motivating plan of *send* that night. Over the years, I've received even more revelation regarding this divine operation and all it entails, but God still hasn't given me utterance for some of the things I've seen.

Recently I was reminded of something a friend of mine related to me in regard to the end-time plan of God. Her sister had gone to heaven and spoken with Jesus. As Jesus talked to this woman, He called this last move of God "the latter rain."

My friend asked her sister, "What does that mean? What is the latter rain?"

Her sister replied, "It is the hour of no impossibilities, in which all things are possible in God."

No Impossibilities in the Book of Acts

The operation of *send* is a part of this present hour of no impossibilities. We can see this divine operation in the book of Acts as well, which records the beginning of the dispensation of the Holy Spirit and revival exploding on the scene. That time period was also marked by an hour of no impossibilities.

How can we describe that moving of God in the book of Acts? We would have to say it was a time when all things were possible with God. That's why it was such a great move.

Just think about the man at the gate Beautiful. (Acts 3:1-8.) That was an impossible situation. Here was a man who had been crippled in his feet his entire life. He had never, ever walked. But when Peter grabbed his hand and pulled him up on his feet in the name of Jesus, he began walking and leaping and praising God. Think about that! Talk about an impossibility!

Now consider Paul and his Damascus-road experience. (Acts 9:1-6.) What an impossible situation that was! Man could never have transformed that zealous persecutor of the church into one of the greatest ministers of the Gospel who ever lived. But Paul's supernatural conversion was absolutely possible with God!

Think about Peter when he raised Dorcas from the dead. (Acts 9:36-41.) Dorcas was a woman who spent her life doing good works and making garments to bless others. As she lay dead in a room with everyone standing around, Peter came in and commanded her to arise—and she did! What could be more impossible with man than raising someone from the dead?

WE ARE BLESSED BECAUSE WE BELIEVE IN THE POWER OF GOD, EVEN THOUGH WE HAVE YET TO SEE THE FULLNESS OF ITS MANIFESTATION.

Move Up to a Higher Level!

You know, within this generation of believers are those of us who don't have "Thomas faith"—in other words, we don't have to see first before we'll believe. We are blessed because we believe in the power of God, even though we have yet to see the fullness of its manifestation. But we're going to! We're going to see the fullness of God's power with our natural eyes!

Now, I'm not trying to minimize what God has already done. I know we all have testimonies of the wonderful works He has done in our lives.

But remember, I'm speaking of *impossibilities* right now. I'm talking about things that in the natural seem "far out"—way beyond what we have yet asked, dreamed or imagined. I'm talking about a higher level of supernatural miracles than most of us have yet experienced or dreamed of. We haven't lifted ourselves up to receive from God at this level. We haven't released our faith to say, "Yes, God, You're going to do that. That impossibility becomes

CLIMB UP TO
THAT HIGHER
LEVEL IN GOD
WHERE *ALL* THINGS
ARE POSSIBLE!

❧

possible through You. I believe it!"

Don't be willing to settle for a lower level of faith in this hour of no impossibilities. It's time to stir yourself up and take your place in God's last-days operation of *send!*

Climb up to that higher level in God where *all* things are possible!

For with God nothing is ever impossible

and no word from God shall be without

power or impossible of fulfillment.

LUKE 1:37

2

CULTIVATE THE FORGOTTEN SEED

2

CULTIVATE THE FORGOTTEN SEED

One night our church family was praying for souls during a prayer meeting. Somehow we got over into praying for hopeless situations—circumstances in which there seems to be no possibility of victory.

As I prayed along this line, I was reminded of some impossibilities that in the past had been strong on my heart. I realized I had really let go of those things; I wasn't believing God for them anymore.

Then God took me to a passage of Scripture that prompted me to take hold of those forgotten desires by faith once more. It was the wonderful account of the angel Gabriel's visit to Mary—a story that will make you fall in love with Jesus all over again!

How, Lord?

Gabriel came to Mary and said, "I've come from the presence of God to give you a message." The message Gabriel brought her was an amazing one: Mary, a young virgin, had been chosen to bear the Son of God!

And the angel said to her, Do not be afraid, Mary, for you have found grace (free, spontaneous, absolute favor and loving-kindness) with God. And listen! You will become pregnant and will give birth to a Son, and you shall call His name Jesus. He will be great (eminent) and will be called the Son of the Most High; and the Lord God will give to Him the throne of His forefather David, And He will reign over the house of Jacob throughout the ages; and of His reign there will be no end.

And Mary said to the angel, How can this be, since I have no [intimacy with any man as a] husband?

Then the angel said to her, The Holy Ghost will come upon you, and the power of the Most High will overshadow you [like a shining cloud]; and so the holy (pure, sinless) Thing (Offspring)

which shall be born of you will be called the Son of God.

And listen! Your relative Elizabeth in her old age has also conceived a son, and this is now the sixth month with her who was called barren. *For with God nothing is ever impossible and no word from God shall be without power or impossible of fulfillment.*

Luke 1:30-37

Now, this is a good example of an impossible situation. Notice Mary's response to Gabriel when he told her that she would bear the Son of God. She asked the angel, *"How?"*

That's an understandable question! How would Mary bear a child when she was still a virgin? Wasn't that an impossibility?

"It will happen *by the Holy Ghost*," Gabriel explained.

If we want to define an impossibility, we could say that it is anything in life that makes us ask God, "*How?* How is this going to come to pass, Lord?" We are speaking of things that absolutely cannot be humanly brought forth.

AN IMPOSSIBILITY IS ANYTHING IN LIFE THAT MAKES US ASK GOD, "*HOW?*"

However, the Bible says that *nothing* is impossible with God! He *always* knows the "how" of every hopeless situation!

Seeds Planted in a Child's Heart

So God was saying to Mary, "A supernatural seed will be conceived on the inside of you, and at the appointed time, the fruit of that divine seed *will* be brought forth."

You know, God is planting supernatural seeds in His people all the time. Just as the Holy Ghost overshadowed Mary and conceived seed within her, God is continually overshadowing His people and putting dreams in their hearts that *shall* be brought forth—dreams that are impossible with man but totally possible with God.

> GOD IS PLANTING SUPERNATURAL SEEDS IN HIS PEOPLE ALL THE TIME.

I still have one of those supernatural, "impossibility" seeds in my heart that the Lord placed there when I was a child before I was even born again. You may ask, "How could He do that?"

I don't know how God did it. But I know He was the One who did it, because I had no environmental or family influence to help me conceive that kind of seed in my heart on my own. I also know part of the reason I got born again was that God kept drawing me through this seed He had planted in my heart.

Sometimes it is a parent or grandparent who plants a seed. For instance, a young girl recently came to talk to me who didn't even know seeds had been planted in her heart by her praying grandmother. The girl said to me, "I have to tell you about a teaching tape I listened to recently. As I was listening, the presence of God took hold of me and I started praying. I've never, ever prayed like that in my whole life! The glory of God just filled my entire being!"

This girl wanted to know what had happened to her, so I talked to her for a while about prayer. "That's really interesting," she said. "You know, my grandmother was a great prayer warrior, and she made such an impression on me in my life. She planted seeds in me that I didn't even know were there until now!"

Uncover the Hidden Seeds in Your Heart

I was talking to a farmer recently, and he said the most interesting thing about seeds. He said, "Some seeds can last up to 100 years in the ground without germinating. Then when the proper conditions and the proper elements are finally present, they will germinate and bring forth life—*just as if they had been planted that very day."*

WHEN THE PROPER CONDITIONS AND THE PROPER ELEMENTS ARE FINALLY PRESENT, SEEDS WILL GERMINATE AND BRING FORTH LIFE.

Now apply those natural facts about seeds to the supernatural seeds God plants in your heart. You see, God is continually dropping seeds into your heart. He may speak to your spirit and give you a dream or a specific assignment—something He wants you to do for Him. Or you may have a calling

GOD IS
CONTINUALLY
DROPPING SEEDS
INTO YOUR HEART.

ℐ•

deep down on the inside of you that you know God has planted there.

But sometimes as the years go by, the "dirt" of life can get pushed over on these divinely planted seeds, hiding them from your view. You may stop thinking about them; you may even allow your heart to grow hard to them. Nevertheless, those forgotten seeds are still in there, waiting for the appointed time to germinate and bring forth a harvest.

Many times on the day He plants that dream or calling in your heart, it goes off like a big explosion! It's so big on the inside of you, it seems like it's going to happen that very day.

But then it *doesn't* happen that day—or the next, or the next. In fact, sometimes your entire life seems to take a completely different direction. You start scratching your head and wondering, *Where did that dream come from? It doesn't fit anything I'm going through right now.*

Maybe you've been pursuing your own plans and purposes, and now you're going a different

MAYBE YOU'VE BEEN PURSUING YOUR OWN PLANS AND PURPOSES, AND NOW YOU'RE GOING A DIFFERENT DIRECTION THAN GOD INTENDED FOR YOU TO GO.

direction than God intended for you to go. As you followed your self-made path, that divine seed got covered up with the cares and worries of this life. Still, every now and then, you remember what God spoke to your heart and you think, *I wonder if that will ever happen.*

SWEEP THE SOIL OFF THOSE SUPERNATURAL SEEDS AND SAY, "YES, I'M GOING TO BELIEVE FOR THAT AGAIN."

If this description fits your life, I want you to start searching for those forgotten seeds you've "swept under the rug." Remind yourself of the "impossible" dreams and desires God has spoken to your heart in times past.

Sweep the soil off those supernatural seeds and say, "Yes, I'm going to believe for that again. More than likely, that was God. He didn't forget about those dreams, because the Holy Ghost is bringing them to my remembrance right now."

I don't know what dreams or divine callings are hidden deep inside of you, but God does. After all, He's the One who put them in there! And you may as well accept this fact: No matter how hard you try to get rid of the seed God has planted inside of you, it's there to stay. That seed in you is

> NO MATTER HOW HARD YOU TRY TO GET RID OF THE SEED GOD HAS PLANTED INSIDE OF YOU, IT'S THERE TO STAY.

NO MATTER HOW DEEP A PIT YOU HAVE DUG FOR YOURSELF, YOU CAN NEVER DIG DEEP ENOUGH TO GET RID OF WHAT GOD HAS PLANTED IN YOUR LIFE!

incorruptible seed, a part of His divine plan for your life. You didn't put it in there, and you can't take it out!

That's actually a wonderful thing to realize. You may have totally messed up your life. You may see yourself as a total loser. But no matter how deep a pit you have dug for yourself, you can never dig deep enough to get rid of what God has planted in your life!

I'm telling you right now that the church of the Lord Jesus Christ is getting ready to bring forth impossibilities that have long been set aside and forgotten. The body of Christ is coming into the right conditions and the right elements for *all* those forgotten seeds to germinate and bring forth a huge harvest for God's kingdom at last!

ALL THINGS ARE POSSIBLE WITH GOD WHERE YOU'RE CONCERNED.

"But how can it happen?" you may ask.

There's only one way any impossibility can become possible—*by the Holy Ghost.* It has to be by the Holy Ghost.

Mark my words, my friend—a tremendous, supernatural harvest of forgotten dreams and hidden callings is about to come forth. And in

the midst of it all, God will be glorified! It is
all part of this hour of no impossibilities.

Determine to be a part of this
unprecedented hour. Cultivate those forgotten
seeds in your own heart by making this your
continual confession: "All things are possible
with God where I'm concerned. God is going
to bring forth every impossible dream or
assignment He has planted in my heart. Those
supernatural seeds are all possible in Him,
and they *will* come forth!"

He said to them, Because of the littleness of your faith [that is, your lack of firmly relying trust]. *For truly I say to you, if you have faith* [that is living] *like a grain of mustard seed, you can say to this mountain, Move from here to yonder place, and it will move; and nothing will be impossible to you.*

MATTHEW 17:20

3

ON THE BRINK OF IMPOSSIBLE BREAKTHROUGHS

3

ON THE BRINK
OF IMPOSSIBLE
BREAKTHROUGHS

Jesus came to this earth to accomplish impossible things—impossible as far as man is concerned, that is. Now, in these last days, He has called us to do even greater works than He did. (John 14:12.) That means we should fully expect God to work through us to make impossibilities possible in this hour!

Physical Impairments Made Whole

I believe we're on the very brink of some breakthroughs in areas we have normally labeled as "impossible." Not long ago, I started to pray along these lines, and the Lord took me to Matthew 17:14-20:

> And when they approached the multitude, a man came up to Him, kneeling before Him and saying, Lord, do pity and have mercy on my son, for he has epilepsy (is moonstruck) and he suffers terribly; for frequently he falls into the fire and many times into the water. And I brought him to Your disciples, and they were not able to cure him.
>
> And Jesus answered, O you unbelieving (warped, wayward, rebellious) and thoroughly perverse generation! How long am I to remain

with you? How long am I to bear with you? Bring him here to Me.

And Jesus rebuked the demon, and it came out of him, and the boy was cured instantly.

Then the disciples came to Jesus and asked privately, Why could we not drive it out? He said to them, Because of the littleness of your faith [that is, your lack of firmly relying trust]. For truly I say to you, if you have faith [that is living] like a grain of mustard seed, you can say to this mountain, Move from here to yonder place, and it will move; and nothing will be impossible to you.

Now, in this account we see that this boy was troubled with some type of demonically inspired seizures. From studying several commentaries, I would also assume that he was mentally retarded in some way.

Notice that the Word of God says the disciples couldn't cast out that demon because of the "littleness" of their faith. Yet Jesus said, "If you have faith that's no bigger than a grain of mustard seed, nothing will be impossible to you!"

> JESUS SAID, "IF YOU HAVE FAITH THAT'S NO BIGGER THAN A GRAIN OF MUSTARD SEED, NOTHING WILL BE IMPOSSIBLE TO YOU!"

Do you know how big a mustard seed is? It's extremely tiny—about the size of the head of a ballpoint pen. But according to Jesus, if you just have faith as big as that tiny grain of mustard seed, you can speak to a mountain in your life, such as an incurable physical condition like epilepsy, and say, "Mountain, *go* in the name of Jesus"—*and it will leave!*

The Lord has put in my heart such a deep compassion for those with physical impairments. I mean, when I see someone who has this kind of physical problem, the compassion of God rises up strong inside of me. I just want to reach out and say, "God, heal that person!"

> WE'RE ON THE BRINK OF A BREAKTHROUGH OF "IMPOSSIBLE" PHYSICAL CONDITIONS.

Remember, Jesus said, "*All* things are possible." I believe we're on the brink of a breakthrough in this area of "impossible" physical conditions. More and more, blind eyes will open, limbs will grow out and the mentally impaired will become absolutely normal. I believe we're going to see all these things as a part of God's plan for this hour.

> LISTEN, MY FRIEND, WE CAN ONLY GO UP FROM HERE. THERE ISN'T ANY WAY BUT UP!

Listen, my friend, we can only go up from here. There isn't any way but up! We're near the end of the age now. We have to lift our faith to a higher level so we can believe God for *whatever* He wants to do *whenever* He wants to do it!

I have a friend whom God gave a tremendous desire to see handicapped people healed during her time of prayer. One day she actually began to see this desire manifested in a vision as she was praying.

In the vision, my friend saw a huge tent with thousands and thousands of people inside enjoying a revival. Then she saw a big section of people on the left side of the platform. Some of these people were deformed; others were severely mentally retarded; all had terrible physical handicaps.

As my friend continued praying, she saw this entire section of handicapped people begin to sing praises to God. Suddenly the Spirit of God began to move like a wind. As that Holy Ghost wind moved across the handicapped section, it instantly healed them and made them whole by the power of God.

You know, when a person sees something like that in the spirit realm, it's easy to take hold of it by faith! But we can also take hold of what God showed my friend that day. We are going to see the impossible take place in regard to incurable physical conditions—and we're going to see it before Jesus comes!

The Wealthy Brought Into God's Kingdom

Now let's go on to another impossibility that is about to be broken in this hour. Jesus talks about it in Mark 10:17-27.

And as He [Jesus] was setting out on His journey, a man ran up and knelt before Him and asked Him, Teacher, [You are essentially and perfectly morally] good, what must I do to

inherit eternal life [that is, to partake of eternal salvation in the Messiah's kingdom]?

And Jesus said to him, Why do you call Me [essentially and perfectly morally] good? There is no one [essentially and perfectly morally] good—except God alone. You know the commandments: Do not kill, do not commit adultery, do not steal, do not bear false witness, do not defraud, honor your father and mother.

And he replied to Him, Teacher, I have carefully guarded and observed all these and taken care not to violate them from my boyhood.

And Jesus, looking upon him, loved him, and He said to him, You lack one thing; go and sell all you have and give [the money] to the poor, and you will have treasure in heaven; and come [and] accompany Me [walking the same road that I walk].

At that saying the man's countenance fell and was gloomy, and he went away grieved and sorrowing, for he was holding great possessions. And Jesus looked around and said to His disciples, With what difficulty will those who possess wealth and keep on holding it enter the kingdom of God?

And the disciples were amazed and bewildered and perplexed at His words. But Jesus said to them again, Children, how hard it is for those who trust (place their confidence, their sense of safety) in riches to enter the kingdom of God! It is easier for a camel to go through the eye of a needle than for a rich man to enter the kingdom of God.

And they were shocked and exceedingly astonished, and said to Him and to one another, Then who can be saved?

Jesus glanced around at them and said, *With men [it is] impossible, but not with God; for all things are possible with God.*

For many years it has been a desire of my heart to see wealthy people come into the kingdom of God. But when the disciples questioned Jesus about this, Jesus said it was next to impossible. He said it was easier for a camel to go through the eye of a needle than for a rich man to be saved!

THE DEVIL USES THAT FALSE FULFILLMENT AND TEMPORARY SATISFACTION TO KEEP THE WEALTHY FROM EVER PRESSING IN TO FIND TRUE SATISFACTION IN JESUS.

Why is that? It's because when rich people become dissatisfied, they begin looking for a false fulfillment instead of reaching for the ultimate source of fulfillment, Jesus Christ. Most of the time, they just go out and purchase something new, which gives them a little temporary satisfaction. The devil uses that false fulfillment and temporary satisfaction to keep them from ever pressing in to find true satisfaction in Jesus.

But I'm telling you, in the last days we are going to see wealthy people—those we might consider the most impossible to win to the Lord—come into the kingdom of God. This is God's plan and His desire, and our faithful prayers can help bring it to pass!

Impossible Doors Opened to the Gospel

In the recent past, we saw the seemingly impossible take place when the eastern bloc countries opened their doors to the Gospel of Jesus Christ. I mean, if you want to talk about an impossibility, that one topped the list! We watched as God worked this incredible, impossible miracle before our very eyes. He demonstrated once and for all that *all* things are possible with Him!

But there are other "impossible" doors to cities and nations that still need to be opened—doors that have long been closed to the Gospel. God wants to supernaturally open doors by His power in these last days.

Many times Paul spoke and prayed along this line. He would talk about effectual doors that were opened for him to preach the Gospel. (1 Cor. 16:9; 2 Cor. 2:12.) He would tell believers, "Pray that a door of utterance would be opened for me in this place." (Col. 4:3.)

ONLY GOD CAN OPEN DOORS FOR US TO REACH OUT INTO OUR COMMUNITY.

You see, in order for us to fulfill God's plans and purposes in this hour, we need doors of impossibility to open for us in different countries, cities and governments. We need some supernatural doors of utterance opened by the power of God!

Only God can open doors for us to reach out into our community and to the ends of this earth with the Gospel. That is a total impossibility with man.

You ought to know that by now. Just count how many people are sitting in the pews of your church Sunday morning, and then compare that number to the population of your city. That should tell you something! It should tell you that there has to be a supernatural working of the Holy Ghost to open every impossible door.

Recently during our church's weekly time of prayer, God led us to pray for crime lords and the Mafia. Wouldn't it be something if God opened *those* impossible doors? Imagine what a testimony to the world it would be if all the members of the Mafia got saved and began testifying all over the world! That would make an awesome front-page headline in the morning newspaper!

WE STAND ON THE VERY BRINK OF SOME AMAZING, SUPERNATURAL BREAKTHROUGHS.

That may sound impossible, but God doesn't see it that way. Jesus said He didn't come for people who were healed and doing well in life. He came for those who needed God (Luke 19:10)—and those who belong to the Mafia, along with millions more people around the world, definitely need God!

We stand on the very brink of some amazing, supernatural breakthroughs. But how can these impossible doors open? How can the physically deformed be made whole? How can the wealthiest billionaires of the world become humble servants in God's kingdom? To every question of "How?" God has one answer, and one answer only: *It's by the Holy Ghost!*

Ask of Me, and I will give You

the nations as Your inheritance,

and the uttermost parts

of the earth as Your possession.

PSALM 2:8

4

AN IMPOSSIBLE HEART TRANSFORMED

4

AN IMPOSSIBLE
HEART TRANSFORMED

Is there anyone in your life who seems like a hopeless case? Maybe you've caught yourself thinking, *That person will never change!* Well, I want to share a testimony with you about someone in my family whom *we* considered a hopeless case. When my sister and I would talk about him, we would look at each other, shake our heads and say, "It's impossible for him to get saved."

But we loved this relative anyway. He was a wonderful person. When our sons were little, we even let them go fishing with him. But whenever we started to talk to this man about Jesus, we could immediately feel the walls going up all around him!

This man just loved to take my sister's three sons and my two sons fishing. So right before the kids left on a fishing trip with him, we would give the children all sorts of ideas about what to say to him regarding the Lord. After all, they would be sitting in the boat with him for a long time!

My sister's youngest son was the boldest of all our children. He has a big dose of fiery evangelism in him! One day during one of those fishing trips, this little four-year-old boy called this man by name and said, "I'm going to tell you right now, if you don't accept Jesus, you're going to burn in hell."

The man put his hands on his hips, looked the little boy straight in the eye and replied, "Well, I'll just have to burn then!"

Do you see why we asked, "How?" whenever we thought about this man getting saved? I mean, it looked like a totally impossible thing!

But remember, this is the hour of no impossibilities! We found that out later, when my brother-in-law and sister started a church. At their second Sunday service, this "hopeless" relative of ours was sitting in the back of the sanctuary. He had come just out of curiosity.

My brother-in-law was preaching on something that didn't even pertain to salvation. But halfway through the message, our relative—who is *not* the type of person to shed tears—began to openly weep!

My sister was sitting on the platform and saw what was happening. She told me later, "My eyes got bigger and bigger as I realized what I was seeing. I even rubbed my eyes and took another look, trying to make sure I was actually seeing that man weep! I thought, *Maybe he's hurting with some kind of pain or something. I wonder if we should pray for him.*"

You see, my sister was thinking, *No way! This is impossible.*

Nevertheless, this man continued to weep all the way through the message. And when my brother-in-law finally gave an altar call for salvation, our relative came weeping to the front and accepted Jesus as his Savior!

As soon as my sister got home from church, she called me on the telephone. Her first words to me struck my heart. She said, "Let me tell you about the most impossible thing that happened today!"

I had already been pondering this subject of impossible things. So when I heard what had occurred in that Sunday service, I thought, *Now, that was an impossible situation!*

We don't even know what happened to change our relative's heart. But God has a way of reaching down into a man's hard heart and

BUT GOD HAS A WAY OF REACHING DOWN INTO A MAN'S HARD HEART AND UNLOCKING THAT IMPOSSIBLE DOOR SO JESUS CAN COME IN!

unlocking that impossible door so Jesus can come in!

What About Your *Impossibilities?*

In conclusion, I want you to think right now of at least one or two impossible things in your own life that cause you to ask the Lord, "How? How can these things come to pass?" It may be a divine call to accomplish something for God. It might be an impossible situation in your home or in your physical health. Whatever your particular impossibilities are, it would be a good idea to write them down along with applicable Scripture promises so you can keep them before your eyes as you stand in faith.

Once I wrote down the names of my unsaved relatives on a sheet of paper and placed the paper right next to Psalm 2:8 KJV, where it says, **Ask of me, and I shall give thee the heathen for thine inheritance.** Every time I'd pass over that page, I'd put my hand on the paper and say, "Father, these are my possession. These are the heathen, and

> WHATEVER YOUR PARTICULAR IMPOSSIBILITIES ARE, IT WOULD BE A GOOD IDEA TO WRITE THEM DOWN ALONG WITH APPLICABLE SCRIPTURE PROMISES.

they are mine. In the name of Jesus, I claim salvation for my family!"

Next, talk to God about these impossibilities. Tell Him, "Lord, I see this situation I wrote down as a total impossibility. But I know through the Word You have given me that all things are possible. I know You will move by Your power when by faith I ask in the name of Jesus.

> SO I ASK YOU, LORD—MAKE MY IMPOSSIBILITIES POSSIBLE! BRING LIFE TO THE FORGOTTEN SEED.

"So I ask You, Lord— make my impossibilities possible! Bring life to the forgotten seed. Heal the impossible physical condition. Open the impossible door.

Melt the impossible heart. My impossible situations are absolutely *possible*, for this is the hour of *no* impossibilities!"

About the Author

Lynne Hammond is nationally known for her teaching and writing on the subject of prayer. The desire of Lynne's heart is to impart the spirit of prayer to churches and nations throughout the world. Her books include *Secrets to Powerful Prayer, When Healing Doesn't Come Easily, Dare To Be Free* and *The Master Is Calling.*

She is the host and teacher for *A Call to Prayer,* a weekly European television broadcast, and is an occasional guest teacher on her husband's national weekly television broadcast, *The Winner's Way With Mac Hammond.* She also regularly writes articles on the subject of prayer in *Winner's Way* magazine and publishes a newsletter called

Prayer Notes for people of prayer. Lynne is a frequent speaker at national prayer conferences and meetings around the country.

Lynne and her husband, Mac, are founders of Living Word Christian Center, a large and growing church in Minneapolis, Minnesota. Under Lynne's leadership at Living Word, the prayer ministry has become a nationally recognized model for developing effective "pray-ers."

To contact Lynne Hammond,
write:

Lynne Hammond

Mac Hammond Ministries

P.O. Box 29469

Minneapolis, Minnesota 55429

*Please include your prayer requests
and comments when you write.*

OTHER BOOKS BY
LYNNE HAMMOND

Spiritual Enrichment Series:
Living in the Presence of God
Heaven's Power for the Harvest
Staying Faith

Secrets to Powerful Prayer:
Discovering the Languages of the Heart

When Healing Doesn't Come Easily

The Master Is Calling:
Discovering the Wonders of Spirit-Led Prayer

Dare To Be Free

Available from your local bookstore.

HARRISON HOUSE
Tulsa, Oklahoma 74153

Prayer of Salvation

God loves you—no matter who you are, no matter what your past. God loves you so much that He gave His one and only begotten Son for you. The Bible tells us that "…whoever believes in him shall not perish but have eternal life" (John 3:16 NIV). Jesus laid down His life and rose again so that we could spend eternity with Him in heaven and experience His absolute best on earth. If you would like to receive Jesus into your life, say the following prayer out loud and mean it from your heart.

Heavenly Father, I come to You admitting that I am a sinner. Right now, I choose to turn away from sin, and I ask You to cleanse me of all unrighteousness. I believe that Your Son, Jesus, died on the cross to take away my sins. I also believe that He rose again from the dead so that I might be forgiven of my sins and made righteous through faith in Him. I call upon the name of Jesus Christ to be the Savior and Lord of my life. Jesus, I choose to follow

You and ask that You fill me with the power of the Holy Spirit. I declare that right now I am a child of God. I am free from sin and full of the righteousness of God. I am saved in Jesus' name. Amen.

If you prayed this prayer to receive Jesus Christ as your Savior for the first time, please contact us on the web at <u>www.harrisonhouse.com</u> to receive a free book.

Or you may write to us at

Harrison House

P.O. Box 35035

Tulsa, Oklahoma 74153

If this book has been a blessing to you
or if you would like to see more of
the Harrison House product line,
please visit us on our website at
www.harrisonhouse.com.

The Harrison House Vision

Proclaiming the truth and the power

Of the Gospel of Jesus Christ

With excellence;

Challenging Christians to

Live victoriously,

Grow spiritually,

Know God intimately.